fondue It!

Silvana Franco

Photographs by
Amanda Heywood

fondue It!

50 Recipes to Dip, Sizzle and Savor

Silvana Franco

Photographs by **Amanda Heywood**

COURAGE BOOKS

AN IMPRINT OF RUNNING PRESS
PHILADELPHIA · LONDON

2002 SALAMANDER BOOKS LTD

Published by Salamander Books Limited

8 Blenheim Court, Brewery Road

London N7 9NY, United Kingdom

9 8 7 6 5 4 3 2

Library of Congress Cataloguing-in-
Publication Number 2001087021

ISBN 0-7624-1157-0

CREDITS

Project management by Anne McDowall
Design by Fiona Roberts of Design Revolution,
Brighton
Edited by Lorraine Turner
Photography by Amanda Heywood
Food styling by Silvana Franco
Photographic styling by Suzy Gittens
Color reproduction by Media Print (UK) Ltd.
Printed and bound in China

This book may be ordered by mail from the publisher.
But try your bookstore first!

This edition published in the United States by
Courage Books, an imprint of
Running Press Book Publishers
125 South Twenty-second Street
Philadelphia, Pennsylvania 19103-4399

Visit us on the web! www.runningpress.com

The author

Silvana Franco is a food writer who regularly contributes to magazines as well as working behind the scenes on popular TV cooking programs. A keen cook and party-thrower, Silvana always has a supply of willing tasters for her home-grown recipes. She lives in London, England, and has written several other cookbooks including *Tapas & Salsas* and *Dips & Relishes*.

The photographer

Amanda Heywood specializes in food photography. She is a keen traveler and has actively sought to use her experiences of different cultures and culinary activities in a new and dynamic approach to her photographs. She has photographed food books for many different publishers and her work has also been included in magazines and campaigns for leading food retailers.

Note

Cup measurements are for American cups. To measure ounces, use a Pyrex cup or similar cup with an ounce listing on the side. All spoon measurements are level. Milk is whole milk and eggs are medium. Because of the slight risk of salmonella, raw eggs should not be served to the very young, the ill or elderly, or to pregnant women.

contents

Introduction

Many people are familiar with the classic cheese fondue and the wonderful combinations that different cheeses, such as colby, Swiss, and Camembert, make with spirits such as brandy. Yet the versatile fondue pot can be put to many other uses.

In this book you will find a multitude of ideas for cooking with your fondue pot. You will be able to make a stockpot, for example, where a fondue pot filled with slowly simmering stock is placed in the center of the table for your guests to dip their own pieces of meat and vegetables into the delicious stock and cook them to their taste. There are also recipes for sizzlers—a faster method of cooking in the fondue pot—where tempting morsels of food are cooked in hot oil. A section is also devoted to an appetizing range of rich sauces and spicy salsas and dips. To crown it all, the sweet fondue section is bursting with irresistible concoctions such as dark chocolate sauce with marinated cherries, and tiramisu fondue with sponge drops. Whether you are cooking an intimate meal for two or entertaining a large group of guests, there are recipes here to delight every palate and suit every occasion.

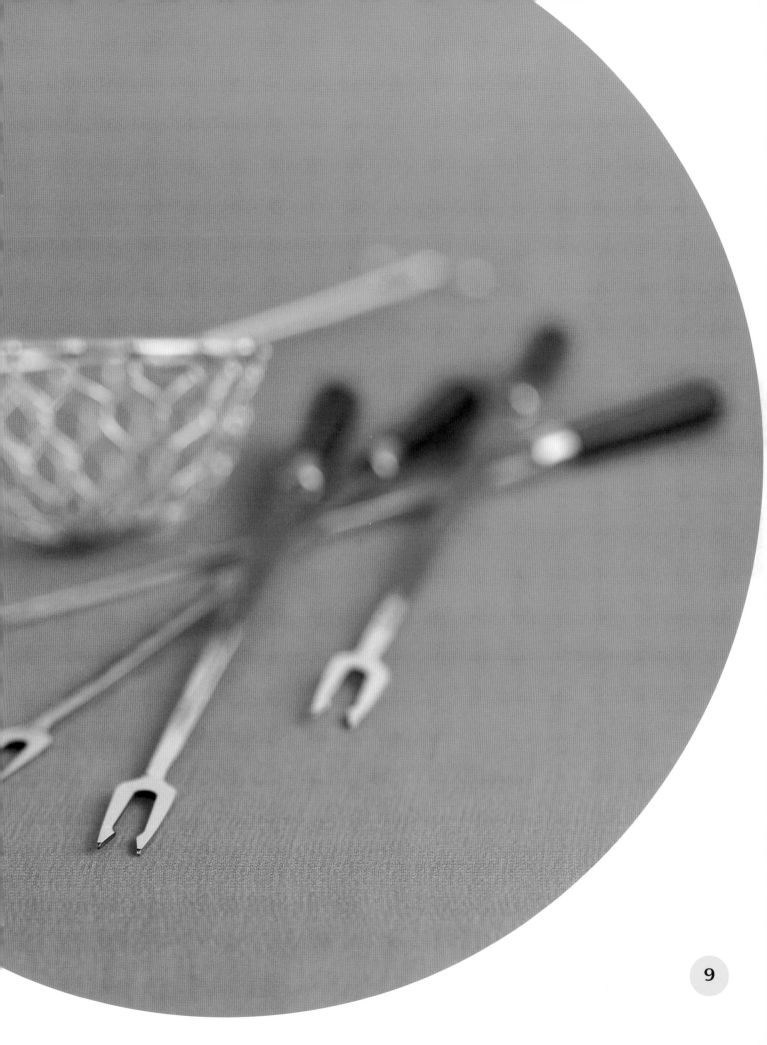

1

Cheese
fondues

Classic Swiss fondue

• **Belgian beer fondue**

• Smoked cheese fondue • The

ultimate fondue • **Wensleydale**

fondue • **Fiery fondue** • Gorgonzola

fonduta • Guinness fondue • Rosé

wine fondue • Spanish fondue

• **Champagne fondue**

The most classic of all
fondues is without doubt the Swiss
cheese fondue. This method of fondue-
making involves melting an amount of cheese
into a pot of warm, garlic-infused wine. A little
cornstarch is then dissolved in a small amount of spirit,
traditionally kirsch (a clear brandy), and then stirred into
the fondue to prevent the cheese from curdling at boiling
point and to thicken the fondue a little. As the fondue
bubbles at the table, it begins to thicken and becomes
increasingly stringy. The thick, golden crust that forms around
the edge and on the bottom of the pot is considered by
many people to be the most enjoyable part of the dish.
Once you have mastered the classic cheese fondue,
you can experiment with endless variations. Always
keep the liquid-to-cheese ratio roughly in
proportion and remember never to boil
the mixture until the cornstarch
has been added.

Classic Swiss fondue

Serves 4

- 1 LARGE GARLIC CLOVE
- 1 CUP PLUS 2 TABLESPOONS DRY WHITE WINE
- 1 TEASPOON FRESH LEMON JUICE
- 7 OUNCES GRUYERE CHEESE (SEE PAGE 22), GRATED
- 7 OUNCES EMMENTAL CHEESE (SEE PAGE 22), GRATED
- 1 TABLESPOON CORNSTARCH
- 1 TABLESPOON KIRSCH OR BRANDY
- SALT AND FRESHLY GROUND WHITE PEPPER
- CUBES OF BREAD AND PICKLED VEGETABLES, TO SERVE

A traditional Swiss fondue is served with cubes of crusty bread, pickled vegetables such as small, sweet gherkins, and a glass of icy kirsch. Kirsch is the traditional spirit used to dissolve the cornstarch added to a classic fondue, but it can be replaced with vodka or regular brandy.

Halve the garlic clove lengthwise and rub the cut surfaces over the bottom and sides of the fondue pot. Add the wine and lemon juice and gently warm through.

Stir in the cheeses and heat gently, stirring until melted, but do not let the mixture boil.

In a separate bowl, dissolve the cornstarch in the kirsch, then stir into the fondue. Slowly bring to a boil, stirring, until thickened. Season to taste, then lower the heat. Serve with cubes of bread and pickles for dipping.

FOOL-PROOF FONDUES

Keep the proportions of cheese to liquid precise • Grate the cheese finely to ensure it melts easily • Let the cheese melt completely before adding the dissolved cornstarch • Do not let the cheese mixture boil before the cornstarch has been added • Beat the cornstarch into the liquid rapidly to avoid lumps, then bring to a boil, stirring constantly, until the mixture has thickened slightly • Cheese tends to be salty, so taste before seasoning • Remember that a fondue often has a slightly uneven texture • If the mixture starts to curdle or separate, beat in some freshly squeezed lemon juice • Remember: the longer the fondue cooks, the more the flavor develops and softens

The traditional way to serve

fondue

13

Belgians love to serve

14

mussels
and fries together

Belgian beer fondue

The Belgians love to serve mussels and french fries together and they do make excellent partners for this tangy fondue. If you're feeling a little adventurous, stir in a dash of cherry schnapps with the cornstarch.

Place the garlic and 1⅓ cups beer in a fondue pot and bring gently to a boil. Lower the heat and simmer gently for 3 to 4 minutes, until the garlic is tender. Add the cheese, stirring until it melts, but take care not to let the mixture boil.

In a separate bowl, dissolve the cornstarch in a little water and pour into the pot. Bring to a boil, stirring continuously, until the sauce is smooth and thickened. Add salt and pepper to taste and keep warm.

Place the mussels, shallot, thyme sprig, 2 tablespoons beer, and plenty of black pepper in a large pan. Cover tightly and steam for around 5 minutes, until all the shells have opened; discard any that remain closed. Remove the thyme sprig, spoon into four individual bowls, and serve immediately with the fondue and hot french fries.

Serves 4

- 2 GARLIC CLOVES, FINELY CHOPPED
- 1⅓ CUPS WHEAT BEER
- 10 OUNCES LIMBURGER CHEESE (SEE PAGE 23), GRATED
- 2 TEASPOONS CORNSTARCH
- SEA SALT AND FRESHLY GROUND WHITE PEPPER
- FRESHLY COOKED FRENCH FRIES, TO SERVE

For the mussels

- 2 POUNDS SMALL MUSSELS, CLEANED
- 1 SHALLOT, FINELY CHOPPED
- 1 SPRIG OF THYME
- 2 TABLESPOONS WHEAT BEER
- FRESHLY GROUND BLACK PEPPER

MAKING FRENCH FRIES

There's nothing worse than soggy, greasy fries and the only way to make sure yours are fluffy in the middle and crisp and golden on the outside is to cook them twice. Choose mealy potatoes rather than waxy new ones and cut the fries fairly thickly. Rinse them well in plenty of cold water, then dry thoroughly on paper towels. Heat the vegetable oil in a deep skillet—it should be hot enough to brown a cube of bread in a minute. Cook the fries for 5 minutes, until lightly golden, then remove with a slotted spoon, and drain on paper towels. When the oil is hot enough to brown a cube of bread in 30 seconds, return the fries to the pan and cook for 2 minutes, until crisp and golden. Drain on paper towels and sprinkle with flaky sea salt.

The **first** choice for most people when it comes to **dippers** for cheese fondues is **bread**. Since it has an absorbent nature and chewy **texture**, **crusty** bread is the **ideal partner for a cheese fondue**, but there are many other suitable **varieties** to choose from, depending on what sort of **cheese fondue** you are planning. Here are some popular ones, but try experimenting with others too.

Rye bread
Rye bread is made with both rye flour and white flour, which give it its distinctive flavor and texture. Light rye breads are at their best a day or two after baking and are very good with pickles, making them a good choice for serving with a classic Swiss fondue.

Bagel
The bagel has an incredibly dense and chewy texture although it is less absorbent than airy breads. The shape of the bagel ring makes it simple to cut for dipping.

Nan
This Indian flat bread is made from a simple dough of white flour and plain yogurt. Traditionally it is cooked in a clay tandoor oven, which few people have at home; fortunately many bakeries and supermarkets stock good-quality, ready-made nan bread.

Choosing bread

Pita bread

Although it is leavened with yeast, pita is a flat bread. During baking it fills with air and puffs up like a balloon, then deflates on cooling, which is why it is easy to split in half with the fingers. It has a distinctive flavor, lovely chewy texture, and can easily be cut into strips for dipping without the need for forks.

Brioche

An enriched, sweet French bread, brioche adds a buttery flavor to savory cheese fondues but is also very good with chocolate and fruit fondues.

Grissini

These crunchy Italian breadsticks can be bought in many different varieties, such as sesame seed or Parmesan. They are also very easy to make at home using a packet of bread dough mix and add a great bite to all cheese fondues.

Baguette

This traditional French stick has a very open and irregularly holed texture and is fairly chewy. It tends to have a hard and shiny crust and, because of its shape, most cubes will have a good, crusty edge when the bread is diced.

Multigrain and nut bread

Cubes of multigrain bread and specialized seed or nut breads offer a delicious, chewy texture and nutty flavor that suit most basic cheese fondues.

Serves 4

- **1** TABLESPOON CORNSTARCH
- **1¼** CUPS MILK
- **10** OUNCES SMOKED CHEESE, GRATED
- **3½** OUNCES SWISS CHEESE, GRATED
- **SALT AND PEPPER**
- **CUBES OF RYE BREAD AND WEDGES OF CRISP, GREEN APPLE, TO SERVE**

Smoked cheese
fondue

This is an alcohol-free fondue with a milk base, so it is not a dish for the purists.

In a bowl, dissolve the cornstarch in 1 to 2 tablespoons of the milk and set aside.

Pour the remaining milk into a fondue pot and heat gently. Add the cheeses and stir until melted, but do not let the mixture boil.

Stir in the cornstarch mixture and bring to a boil, stirring until thickened. Season to taste and serve with the bread cubes and apple wedges, for dipping.

Rich and delicious fondues for every occasion

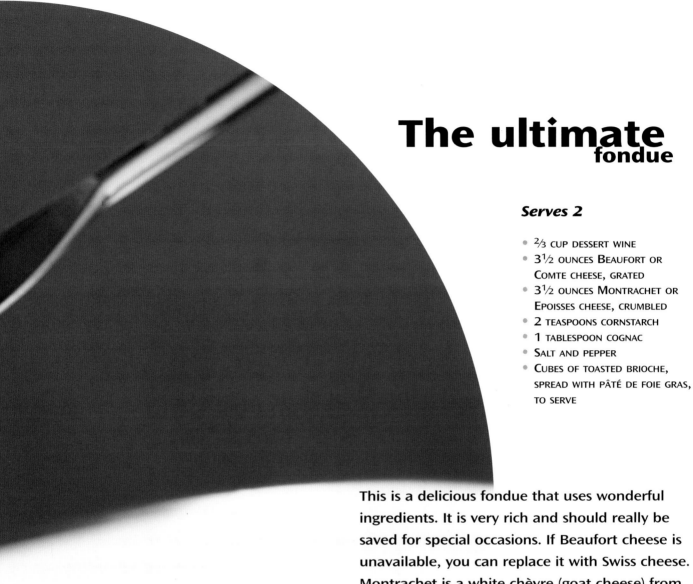

The ultimate fondue

Serves 2

- ⅔ cup dessert wine
- 3½ ounces Beaufort or Comte cheese, grated
- 3½ ounces Montrachet or Epoisses cheese, crumbled
- 2 teaspoons cornstarch
- 1 tablespoon cognac
- Salt and pepper
- Cubes of toasted brioche, spread with pâté de foie gras, to serve

This is a delicious fondue that uses wonderful ingredients. It is very rich and should really be saved for special occasions. If Beaufort cheese is unavailable, you can replace it with Swiss cheese. Montrachet is a white chèvre (goat cheese) from Burgundy. If you have difficulty finding it, you can use any soft, white, tangy goat cheese instead.

Pour the wine into the fondue pot and heat gently. Add the cheeses and stir until melted, but do not let the mixture boil.

In a separate bowl, dissolve the cornstarch in the brandy, then add the mixture to the fondue. Bring to a boil, stirring until thickened. Season to taste, then serve with the brioche cubes.

If you cannot find Wensleydale in your local store, you can buy it through mail order. Try Infood in Tenafly, New Jersey, at 201 569 3175, or visit their website at www.somerdale.u-net.com/wensleydale.html.

Grainy Wensleydale
fondue

In a bowl, dissolve the cornstarch in 1 to 2 tablespoons of the ale and set aside.

Pour the remaining ale into a fondue pot and heat gently. Add the cheese and stir until melted, but do not boil. Add the mustard and the cornstarch and bring to a boil, stirring until thickened.

Season to taste and serve with the chipolata sausages and pickled onions, for dipping.

Serves 4

- 1 TABLESPOON CORNSTARCH
- 1 CUP PLUS 2 TABLESPOONS REAL ALE (STRONG MALT BEER), SUCH AS BASS ALE OR CAFFREY'S IRISH ALE
- 14 OUNCES WENSLEYDALE CHEESE, FINELY CRUMBLED
- 2 TABLESPOONS WHOLEGRAIN MUSTARD
- SALT AND PEPPER
- COOKED CHIPOLATA SAUSAGES, AND PICKLED PEARL ONIONS, TO SERVE

Exciting flavors to tempt the palate

Vodka is a colorless, almost tasteless, grain-based spirit, which goes well with added flavorings. Popular flavorings include fruits, such as lemon and raspberry, and hot chile peppers.

Serves 4

- 1 GARLIC CLOVE, CRUSHED
- 2 SMALL, RED CHILE PEPPERS, SEEDED AND FINELY CHOPPED
- 1 CUP PLUS 2 TABLESPOONS WHITE WINE
- 7 OUNCES SWISS CHEESE, GRATED
- 1 TEASPOON ENGLISH MUSTARD POWDER (SEE BELOW)
- 7 OUNCES SHARP CHEESE, GRATED
- 1 TABLESPOON CORNSTARCH
- 2 TABLESPOONS LEMON VODKA
- SALT AND PEPPER
- STRIPS OF TOASTED PITA, AND FRESH STRAWBERRIES AND GRAPES, TO SERVE

Fiery fondue

If you cannot find English mustard powder in your local store, try telephoning The Spice House at 312 274 0378, or log onto www.thespicehouse.com.

Place the garlic, chile peppers, and wine in a fondue pot and heat gently. Add the cheese and mustard, and stir until melted, but do not let the mixture boil.

In a separate bowl, dissolve the cornstarch in the vodka and add the mixture to the fondue. Bring to a boil, stirring, until thickened. Season to taste and serve with the pita strips and fruit.

If you cannot find these cheeses, the following suppliers stock European cheeses, including Italian mascarpone. Call igourmet toll-free at 1 877 446 8763 (www.igourmet.com) or try Delicious Orchards at (732) 462 1989 (www.deliciousorchardsnj.com).

Gruyère
The second most famous Swiss cheese, Gruyère is also fairly mild but with a dense, small-holed texture. It melts well, giving the classic fondue its lovely stretchy consistency.

Fontina cheese
Fontina is an alpine cheese and is made with unpasteurized cow's milk. It has a delicate flavor and forms the base of the Italian fondue called "fonduta."

Camembert
One of Normandy's most popular cheeses, Camembert is well known for its oozing, melting qualities. Derind it before adding it to the fondue pot.

Emmental
With its large airholes and rich, buttery-yellow coloring, Emmental is a typical Swiss cheese. It has a mellow, mildly nutty flavor and melts marvelously.

Manchego
Manchego is a famous Spanish cheese. It is rich and golden, with a full, mellow flavor, and melts beautifully.

Smoked cheese
The delicious, smoky flavor of smoked cheese is ideal for fondues. Many smoked cheeses are available, including Swiss, Cheddar, Gouda, and goat cheese.

Cheese for fondues

Limburger
Traditional Limburger is a very strong Belgian cheese. If you find it difficult to obtain, or if you prefer something a little more mellow, you can opt for a milder, but still flavorsome, alternative from a neighboring country, such as a Dutch Gouda or a Swiss Emmental.

Wensleydale
This mild, milky cheese (see page 20) has a soft, crumbly texture that melts well. It is good with pickles and bread.

Bleu cheese
Mild bleu cheeses such as dolcelatte, cashel blue, or mycella have a good flavor and work very well in fondues when paired with a waxy cheese such as Gruyère.

Soft goat cheese
Known by the all-encompassing label "chèvre," soft goat cheeses such as Montrachet and crottin add a delicious and distinctive flavor to otherwise simple fondues.

Cheddar
This is Britain's most popular cheese. A sharp, farmhouse Cheddar has a full-bodied flavor that works very well in fondues. Avoid the mild Cheddars that offer little by way of flavor.

Gorgonzola fonduta
with grilled polenta

Polenta makes a lovely dipper for this full-bodied fondue. Warm it right through before serving.

Pour the wine into the fondue pot and heat gently. Add the cheese and heat gently, stirring until melted, but do not let the mixture boil. In a separate bowl, dissolve the cornstarch in the vodka and add to the fondue. Bring to a boil, stirring, until thickened. Season to taste.

On the stove, bring the salted water to a boil in a pan and pour in the polenta in a slow, steady stream, stirring until thick and lump-free. Beat in the olives, sun-dried tomatoes, Parmesan, and butter. Pour the polenta onto an oiled cookie sheet and spread with a spatula to a 3/4-inch thickness.

Cut the polenta into triangles and brush with olive oil. Cook in a hot griddle pan for 2 to 3 minutes on each side, until crisp and golden brown. Serve with the fondue.

Serves 4

- 1 CUP PLUS 2 TABLESPOONS WHITE WINE
- 7 OUNCES FONTINA CHEESE, FINELY CHOPPED
- 7 OUNCES GORGONZOLA CHEESE, CRUMBLED
- 1 TABLESPOON CORNSTARCH
- 2 TABLESPOONS VODKA
- SALT AND PEPPER

For the polenta

- 2½ CUPS BOILING, SALTED WATER
- 6 OUNCES INSTANT POLENTA
- 3½ OUNCES STRONG, BLACK OLIVES, PITTED AND FINELY CHOPPED
- 6 SUN-DRIED TOMATOES IN OIL, DRAINED AND FINELY CHOPPED
- 4 TABLESPOONS FRESHLY GRATED PARMESAN CHEESE
- 1 TEASPOON BUTTER
- OLIVE OIL, FOR BRUSHING

POLENTA
Polenta is a fine cornmeal from northern Italy. It is now available in "instant" form, which means the laborious stirring and bubbling of raw polenta can now be avoided without losing the good quality of the end result. In Italy, the cooked, wet polenta mixture is often flavored with butter and cheese and served with a hearty sauce or as an accompaniment to an entrée, similar to mashed potatoes. The mixture sets rapidly on cooling and can be sliced into pieces and griddled or sautéed, as in this recipe.

This may appear to be a bizarre combination, but the teaming of English Cheddar cheese (see page 23) and Guinness, with the newly available Irish spirit Poitin, is an absolute winner.

Pour the Guinness into a fondue pot and heat gently. Add the cheese and stir until melted, but do not let the mixture boil.

In a separate bowl, dissolve the cornstarch in the Poitin, then add it to the fondue. Bring to a boil, stirring until thickened. Season to taste and serve with the soda bread chunks.

Serves 4

- 1⅓ cups canned Guinness
- 1 pound Wexford Cheddar cheese, or other Irish Cheddar, finely grated
- 1 tablespoon cornstarch
- 2 tablespoons Poitin (see below)
- Salt and pepper

To serve
- Chunks of soda bread
- Slices of blood sausage, sautéed (optional)

POITIN

This is an Irish spirit, which has been illegally distilled from potatoes since the nineteenth century. However, it is at long last commercially available under the brand name "Hackler," among others, and is very smooth with a delicious, mild, vanilla flavor. If you cannot find Poitin, use vodka instead.

Rosé wine fondue

This is a very sophisticated fondue, perfect for a romantic supper or candlelit dinner party.

Cut the garlic clove in half lengthwise and rub the cut surfaces over the bottom and sides of the fondue pot. Add the wine and lemon juice and stir over a low heat, until warm but not boiling.

Stir in the cheeses and continue to heat, stirring, until melted. Do not let the mixture boil or it will separate.

In a separate bowl, dissolve the cornstarch in the kirsch and stir it into the fondue. Slowly bring to a boil, stirring, until the mixture thickens. Season to taste, lower the heat, and sprinkle over the peppercorns.

Cut the prosciutto into strips 3/4 inch wide and wrap around the grissini breadsticks. Tuck a small basil leaf between the overlapping layers of ham so that each stick has two leaves, then serve for dipping.

Serves 4

- 1 LARGE GARLIC CLOVE
- 1 CUP PLUS 2 TABLESPOONS ROSÉ WINE
- 1 TEASPOON FRESH LEMON JUICE
- 7 OUNCES SWISS CHEESE, GRATED
- 7 OUNCES CHEDDAR CHEESE, GRATED (SEE PAGE 23)
- 1 TABLESPOON CORNSTARCH
- 1 TABLESPOON KIRSCH OR BRANDY
- SALT AND FRESHLY GROUND WHITE PEPPER
- A FEW PINK PEPPERCORNS (SEE BELOW)
- PROSCIUTTO, GRISSINI BREADSTICKS, AND FRESH BASIL LEAVES, TO SERVE

PINK PEPPERCORNS

Pink peppercorns are tiny dried berries, and have a sweet, delicate flavor. If you use a pepper mill, add a teaspoon of ground pink peppercorns to your regular variety of peppercorns for an attractive appearance and added flavor. Pink peppercorns can be found in gourmet stores.

Serves 4

- 1 CUP PLUS 2 TABLESPOONS SPANISH WHITE WINE
- 14 OUNCES MANCHEGO CHEESE (SEE PAGE 22)
- 1 TABLESPOON CORNSTARCH
- 2 TABLESPOONS DRY SHERRY
- SALT AND PEPPER

To serve

- TAPAS SUCH AS BREADSTICKS, CUBES OF TORTILLA (SPANISH OMELET), SPICY POTATOES, AND BANDERILLAS (SKEWERS OF PICKLES)
- 3½ OUNCES SERRANO HAM, SHREDDED

Spanish fondue

Pour the wine into a fondue pot and heat gently. Add the cheese and stir over low heat until melted, but do not let the mixture boil.

In a separate bowl, dissolve the cornstarch in the sherry, then add it to the fondue. Bring to a boil, stirring, until thickened. Season to taste. Serve with a selection of tapas, wrapped in strips of serrano ham.

Delicious morsels dipped in mouthwatering flavors

Champagne _fondue_

Pour the Champagne into a fondue pot and heat gently. Add the cheeses and stir over low heat until melted, but do not let the mixture boil.

In a separate bowl, dissolve the cornstarch in the brandy and add it to the fondue. Bring to a boil, stirring, until thickened. Season to taste and serve with the French bread and salami chunks, for dipping.

Serves 4

- 1 cup plus 2 tablespoons Champagne or fine sparkling wine
- 7 ounces soft goat cheese, crumbled
- 7 ounces Camembert, derinded and thinly sliced
- 1 tablespoon cornstarch
- 2 tablespoons French brandy
- Salt and pepper
- Cubes of crunchy French baguette and chunks of salami, to serve

31

2 Stockpots

Pumpkin and Parmesan gnocchi

• Hot and sour Szechuan noodles

• Seafood stockpot • Vegetarian ramen with pickled cucumber • Pot sticker dumplings • Moroccan-style chicken • Poached eggs and asparagus with hollandaise sauce • Thai-style duck stockpot • Skewered chicken spirals • Jumbo shrimp ravioli with infused oil • Mixed won ton

A stockpot is a very modern, health-conscious way to enjoy fondues. The fondue pot is filled with a delicious broth or stock in which raw ingredients or prepared dishes, such as Chinese pot sticker dumplings, are cooked. Here the influence is very Asian with the dish taking its flavor from ingredients such as bok choy and five-spice powder. A few of the dishes are also Mediterranean-inspired, including favorites like gnocchi and ravioli. Stockpot cooking may take a little longer than other fondue methods because the food is cooked at a gentle simmer rather than in the fierce heat of the sizzling dishes. In many of the recipes, the fragrant stock is served as part of the dish, like a soup base. Most of these dishes are served with steamed rice or noodles.

The secret to achieving light and fluffy gnocchi is to try to keep the amount of flour to a minimum. There are many factors that will affect the amount of flour you need, so it is best to add it very gradually and stop when the mixture is just firm enough to shape.

Roast, steam, boil, or microwave the pumpkin and garlic until tender. Place in a food processor with the basil and blend to make a smooth purée. Transfer to a large bowl, and let cool.

Beat the ricotta, Parmesan, and plenty of salt and pepper into the cooled purée. Gradually add enough flour to make a soft dough. Pull off small pieces of dough and roll into lozenge shapes, then roll each lozenge across the back of a fork to make light ridges. Place the gnocchi on individual plates greased with a little olive oil.

Cook the gnocchi in the gently simmering stock in a fondue pot for 4 to 5 minutes until they float on the surface. Remove from the stockpot and top with a teaspoon of butter, a sprinkling of Parmesan, and a little black pepper.

Serves 6

- 1 SMALL PUMPKIN OR BUTTERNUT SQUASH, SKINNED, SEEDED AND CUBED
- 3 GARLIC CLOVES
- LARGE HANDFUL FRESH BASIL LEAVES
- 1 POUND 2 OUNCES RICOTTA CHEESE
- 2¾ OUNCES PARMESAN CHEESE, FRESHLY GRATED, PLUS EXTRA TO SERVE
- SALT AND FRESHLY GROUND BLACK PEPPER
- 1 CUP ALL-PURPOSE FLOUR
- OLIVE OIL, FOR GREASING
- 2½ CUPS HOT VEGETABLE STOCK, FOR POACHING (SEE BASIC STOCKS, PAGES 36 TO 37)
- 1 TEASPOON BUTTER, TO SERVE

Gently simmering dishes
to delight the senses

The recipes in this chapter call for **light, flavorsome** stock rather than the rich, dark stocks of the **traditional** French chef, so the cooking times are kept fairly short. For a **successful**, clean-tasting **stock**, always use **fresh** ingredients and take care not to overboil the stock because this can give a cloudy result. Once boiling point has been reached, keep the stock at a gentle simmer, and regularly skim the surface for a clear broth.

Chicken stock

Makes 4¹⁄₂ cups

Meat stock can be made in the same way as this stock, using fleshy bones instead of a small chicken carcass.

- 2 TABLESPOONS VEGETABLE OIL
- 1 SMALL ONION, ROUGHLY CHOPPED
- 2 CELERY STALKS, ROUGHLY CHOPPED
- 1 CARROT, ROUGHLY CHOPPED
- 4 OR 5 NAPA CABBAGE LEAVES, ROUGHLY CHOPPED
- 2 CUPS WATER
- 1 SMALL CHICKEN CARCASS, ROUGHLY BROKEN

On a stove, heat the oil in a large pan and cook the vegetables for 10 minutes, until softened but not colored. Stir in the water and the chicken carcass and bring to a boil. Simmer over low heat for 1¹⁄₂ hours. Pass through a fine strainer and chill.

Vegetable stock

Makes 4½ cups

- 2 TABLESPOONS VEGETABLE OIL
- 1 SMALL ONION, ROUGHLY CHOPPED
- 1 SMALL LEEK, ROUGHLY CHOPPED
- 2 CELERY STALKS, ROUGHLY CHOPPED
- 1 CARROT, ROUGHLY CHOPPED
- 2 TOMATOES, ROUGHLY CHOPPED
- 5 CUPS WATER
- 1 BAY LEAF, OR 1 SPRIG OF THYME OR ROSEMARY
- 2 OR 3 SPRIGS OF PARSLEY

On a stove, heat the vegetable oil in a large pan. Gently cook the onion and leek for 2 to 3 minutes. Add the remaining vegetables and cook over low heat for 10 minutes, until softened but not colored. Add the water and herbs; bring to a boil. Lower the heat and simmer gently for 20 minutes. Pass through a fine strainer and chill until ready to use.

Basic Stocks

Fish stock

Makes 4½ cups

- 2 TABLESPOONS VEGETABLE OIL
- 1 SMALL ONION, ROUGHLY CHOPPED
- ½ FENNEL BULB, ROUGHLY CHOPPED
- 1 SMALL LEEK, ROUGHLY CHOPPED
- 5 CUPS WATER
- 2 POUNDS WHITE FISH BONES AND TRIMMINGS, ROUGHLY CHOPPED
- HANDFUL FRESH DILL OR CHERVIL
- 5 TABLESPOONS WHITE WINE

On a stove, heat the oil in a large pan. Cook the vegetables for 10 minutes, until softened but not colored. Stir in the remaining ingredients. Bring to a boil, then simmer over low heat for 20 minutes. Strain, and chill.

Dashi

Makes 4½ cups

Dashi is a light, Japanese-style fish stock that is simple to make if you can find the ingredients. Do not let the bonito flakes stay in the pan too long or the stock will become bitter.

- 4½ CUPS WATER
- 1 OUNCE KOMBU SEAWEED
- 1 OUNCE BONITO (DRIED FISH) FLAKES

On a stove, pour the water into a large pan. Add the seaweed and heat gently. As it reaches boiling point, add the bonito flakes. Strain immediately, then chill until ready to use.

Hot and sour Szechuan noodles

The Szechuan peppercorns add a delicious lemon flavor to this noodle soup.

Place the shiitake mushrooms in a large bowl and pour over the boiling water. Let soak for 20 minutes. Remove the mushrooms with a slotted spoon. Reserve the liquid and slice the mushrooms.

Drain the mushroom stock through cheesecloth into a large fondue pot. Add the ginger, chile peppers, garlic, and mushrooms and bring to a boil. Lower the heat and simmer for 3 to 4 minutes.

In a separate bowl, stir together the sugar, vinegar, soy sauce, sesame oil, and Szechuan pepper. Pour the mixture into the fondue and cook for another 1 to 2 minutes.

Quickly reheat the cooked noodles in the Szechuan soup and divide between four bowls. Cook the pork and vegetables in the soup until tender, then lift them out with a slotted spoon, and place on top of the noodles. Spoon over some of the soup and sprinkle with scallions and cilantro.

Serves 4

For the soup
- 1¼ ounces dried shiitake (golden oak) mushrooms
- 6⅓ cups boiling water
- 1¼-inch piece fresh gingerroot, cut into matchsticks
- 2 fresh red chile peppers, seeded and sliced lengthwise into matchsticks
- 2 garlic cloves, finely chopped
- 1 teaspoon superfine sugar
- 4 tablespoons rice vinegar (see page 68)
- 4 tablespoons soy sauce
- 2 teaspoons sesame oil
- 2 teaspoons ground Szechuan pepper (see stock flavorings, pages 42 to 43)

For the table
- 8 cups cooked udon noodles (see page 51)
- 10 ounces pork fillet (tenderloin), cut into strips ½ inch wide
- 8 ounces canned bamboo shoots, drained
- 8 ounces bean sprouts
- 8 ounces snow peas

To garnish
- 4 scallions, shredded into 1½-inch lengths
- 4 tablespoons chopped fresh cilantro

Delicious **fondues** cooked and served **Asian-style**

Seafood stockpot

This seafood stockpot can be served with freshly cooked pasta as shown here, but is also delicious with noodles, plain rice, or just crusty bread and a crisp green salad.

Pour the stock into a fondue pot and add the garlic and chile peppers. Bring to a gentle simmer and cook over low heat for 2 to 3 minutes.

If you are using a mixture of raw and cooked seafood, add the raw seafood first and poach for 2 minutes, then add the cooked seafood and simmer for another 2 to 3 minutes until very hot.

In a separate large bowl, stir together the drained hot tagliatelle, a good dash of olive oil, the chopped herbs, and plenty of black pepper. Lift out the seafood with a slotted spoon, arrange it over the tagliatelle, and pour over a little of the cooking stock.

Serves 4

- 2½ CUPS HOT, FRESH FISH STOCK, FOR POACHING (SEE BASIC STOCKS, PAGES 36 TO 37)
- 2 LARGE GARLIC CLOVES, THINLY SLICED
- 2 RED CHILE PEPPERS, SEEDED AND THINLY SLICED

For the table

- 12 RAW JUMBO SHRIMP, SHELLED AND DEVEINED
- 3½ OUNCES SQUID RINGS
- 8 LARGE GREEN-LIPPED MUSSELS
- 8 SCALLOPS
- 4 CRACKED CRAB CLAWS

To serve

- 14 CUPS HOT, FRESHLY COOKED TAGLIATELLE, OR OTHER RIBBON PASTA
- DASH EXTRA-VIRGIN OLIVE OIL
- 2 TABLESPOONS CHOPPED FRESH PARSLEY OR BASIL
- FRESHLY GROUND BLACK PEPPER

When making a stockpot, the fondue pot is filled with a delicious broth or stock in which a variety of raw ingredients or prepared dishes are cooked. In many **stockpot** recipes, the influence is very Asian, with the dish taking its flavor from ingredients such as **ginger, lemongrass, bok choy, five-spice powder,** and **shrimp paste.** A homemade stock is hard to beat. Fresh vegetables, herbs, and fragrant additions such as fish sauce and fresh lime juice offer a vibrant complexity of flavors that commercially-bought varieties cannot match. A good stock should be **clear,** not cloudy, but can range from a colorless or pale liquid to one that is a rich, dark brown. Once it has been used to cook the ingredients, the clean-tasting liquid can be ladled into the serving bowl as a **delicious broth.** Most of the stocks used in the recipes in this chapter take a relatively short time to prepare, can be made several hours ahead of time, and also freeze very well. The following ingredients all make excellent **flavorings** for the stock.

Cilantro

The fresh leaves and stalks of cilantro have an aromatic flavor that adds a delicate touch to many light stock bases.

Bonito flakes

Along with kombu, this makes up the base of *dashi*, the classic Japanese soup base. Bonito is a dried fish that can bought from specialty stores in wafer-thin flakes.

Fish sauce

This is a thin, salty condiment which is made from fermented fish. It has a strong, surprisingly not-too-fishy flavor and is added to stocks in fairly small quantities. It is used extensively in Thai (*nam pla*) and Vietnamese (*nuoc mam*) cooking.

Szechuan pepper

To get the best flavor, grind the peppercorns yourself: pound them in a mortar and pestle to separate the pepper from the papery husks, then pass the pepper through a fine strainer to remove the husks.

Chile peppers

The fiery heat of a chile pepper enlivens most stocks. Choose fresh or dried but use sparingly.

Shrimp paste

A compressed, dried paste made simply from pounded shrimp, this is an essential Thai-style flavoring.

Stock flavorings

Garlic

The essential Mediterranean ingredient, garlic has a unique flavor, which will ensure that it find its way into most stock bases.

Kombu

This is a type of kelp seaweed that is sold dried in Asian food stores. It has a very good flavor and is an invaluable ingredient in Japanese stocks.

Miso

Miso is a thick paste made from fermented soy beans. It has a delicious, savory flavor and is the base of Japanese miso soup.

Ginger

Fresh gingerroot adds a warm, fragrant flavor to stock. The young root can be bought thinly sliced and pickled and has a sweet, delicate flavor that is often used in Japanese cooking.

Thai curry paste

This is a wet paste made from aromatic ingredients including ginger, garlic, lemon grass, chile peppers, and shrimp paste. It is easy to make but good-quality commercial varieties are now available.

Soy sauce

This sweet, salty sauce is made from soy beans and roasted grains, and is fermented in oak casks for several months. Soy sauce is a great addition to all Asian stocks, and is also a valuable table condiment. There are many different types, of varying ages and thicknesses, including *tamari*, *shoyu*, and the fabulous Indonesian soy sauce *kecap manis*.

Mirin

Mirin is a sweet, syrupy saké (Japanese wine) used for cooking. It is a great addition to many marinades and stocks.

Lemongrass

As its name implies, lemongrass does indeed have a delicate, lemon flavor. The thick, woody stalk should be lightly crushed with a rolling pin to release the flavors. Lemongrass is a very important Southeast Asian ingredient, and can now be bought from specialty stores and supermarkets.

Coconut milk

Coconut milk is available in stores and supermarkets as canned milk, and is an invaluable ingredient when preparing creamy Thai-style soups and curry bases.

Vegetarian ramen with pickled cucumber

Serves 4

For the pickled cucumber
- 1/2 CUCUMBER
- 3 TABLESPOONS RICE VINEGAR (SEE PAGE 68)
- 1 TABLESPOON MIRIN (SEE PAGE 43)
- 1/4 TEASPOON CHILI FLAKES
- 1/2 TEASPOON SALT

For the teriyaki sauce
- 4 TABLESPOONS SOY SAUCE
- 4 TABLESPOONS SAKÉ (JAPANESE WINE)
- 4 TABLESPOONS MIRIN
- 1 TEASPOON SUPERFINE SUGAR

For the table
- 8 CUPS COOKED EGG NOODLES
- 2½ CUPS HOT, FRESH VEGETABLE STOCK, FOR POACHING (SEE BASIC STOCKS, PAGES 36 TO 37)
- 2 OUNCES AUBERAGE (SEE BELOW), CUT INTO STRIPS 1½ INCHES WIDE
- 5 OUNCES SMALL MUSHROOMS, SLICED
- 10 OUNCES NAPA CABBAGE OR FRESH SPINACH LEAVES

This ramen (Japanese-style noodle soup) is made with teriyaki sauce, which is a simple mixture of soy sauce, saké, and mirin (see stock flavorings, pages 42 to 43). If you want to save time, good-quality teriyaki sauces are available from large supermarkets.

To make the pickled cucumber, halve the cucumber lengthwise and scoop out the seeds with a teaspoon. Thinly slice into half-moons and place in a bowl with the rice vinegar, mirin, and chili flakes. Toss well together, cover with plastic wrap, and chill for 20 to 30 minutes.

In a separate bowl, stir together the teriyaki sauce ingredients in a fondue pot. Briefly reheat the noodles in the hot stock, remove with a slotted spoon, and divide between four bowls.

Poach the auberage in the stock for 1 minute, remove with a slotted spoon, and place on top of the noodles. Next poach the mushrooms for 2 to 3 minutes, until tender; remove with a slotted spoon and place next to the auberage. Cook the napa cabbage for 2 to 3 minutes until wilted, then remove with a slotted spoon. Place a neat pile of cabbage on top of each bowl of noodles.

Stir the teriyaki sauce into the stock and heat through. Pour the hot soup over the noodles, top each bowl with a pile of pickled cucumber, and serve.

AUBERAGE
The auberage used in this recipe is a very light, deep-fried bean curd. It comes in thin, rectangular sheets and is usually frozen. If you have difficulty finding it, you can make it yourself. Slice a block of firm bean curd horizontally into ½-inch thick slices. Heat 1½ inches of vegetable oil in a deep skillet and cook the bean curd for 3 to 5 minutes, until crisp and golden. Drain the bean curd on paper towels.

Place the flour in a food processor and, with the motor running, gradually add 4 to 5 tablespoons of warm water to make a soft, pliable dough. Using a pasta machine, roll out the dough as thinly as possible. Stamp out 24 circles with a 3-inch cookie cutter.

In a large bowl, mix together the pork, five-spice powder, scallions, garlic, cilantro, Tabasco sauce, and seasoning. Divide the mixture between the dough circles, moisten the edges with water, and bring together to enclose the filling.

Brush a flat griddle or a heavy-bottomed skillet with a little oil and heat until very hot. Cook the dumplings for 30 seconds on each side, until just tinged with brown.

In a bowl, stir together the dipping sauce ingredients. Gently cook the dumplings in the stock in a fondue pot for 5 minutes; lift them out. Cook the bok choy in the stockpot for 2 minutes, lift it out, and serve with the dumplings and dipping sauce.

Serves 6

- 1¼ cups all-purpose flour
- 3½ ounces ground pork
- 1 teaspoon five-spice powder
- 4 scallions, finely chopped
- 2 garlic cloves, finely chopped
- 2 tablespoons chopped fresh cilantro
- Few drops Tabasco sauce
- Salt and freshly ground black pepper
- Vegetable oil, for brushing
- Hot chicken stock, for poaching (see basic stocks, pages 36 to 37)
- 6 small heads bok choy

For the dipping sauce
- 2 tablespoons dark soy sauce
- 1 tablespoon rice wine vinegar
- Few drops chili oil

BOK CHOY

This mild and versatile vegetable is also known as pak choi, Chinese white cabbage, and white mustard cabbage. Bok choy is related to Chinese (napa) cabbage, but should not be confused with it. Bok choy looks like a bunch of wide-stalked celery because it has crisp, white stalks and long, full, dark-green leaves. It can be used raw in salads, or cooked as a vegetable. It is sold all year round in many supermarkets, and will keep, airtight, in the refrigerator for 3 to 4 days. When buying bok choy, choose bunches with firm, white stalks and crisp, green

47

Moroccan-style chicken

Mix together the spices and salt and sprinkle over the chicken. Cover with plastic wrap and set aside for 1 hour.

Place the chicken in the fondue pot with the hot chicken stock, garlic, cilantro, lemon juice, tomatoes, and olives and simmer gently for 20 minutes, until the chicken is cooked through.

Divide the steamed couscous between four serving bowls. Using a slotted spoon, lift out the chicken and place it on the couscous, then pour over some of the cooking liquid. Top each bowl with a small spoonful of the harissa sauce and eat immediately.

Serves 4

- 1 TEASPOON GROUND CUMIN
- 1 TEASPOON GROUND PAPRIKA
- 1/4 TEASPOON TURMERIC
- 1/4 TEASPOON CAYENNE PEPPER
- 1/2 TEASPOON SALT
- 8 SKINLESS, BONELESS CHICKEN THIGHS
- 2 1/2 CUPS HOT CHICKEN STOCK (SEE BASIC STOCKS, PAGES 36 TO 37)
- 2 GARLIC CLOVES, THINLY SLICED
- 4 TABLESPOONS ROUGHLY CHOPPED FRESH CILANTRO
- JUICE OF 2 LEMONS
- 4 TOMATOES, ROUGHLY CHOPPED
- 3 1/2 OUNCES PITTED BLACK OLIVES
- STEAMED COUSCOUS, AND HARISSA SAUCE, TO SERVE

HARISSA SAUCE

This fiery-hot sauce is a pungent condiment that comes from Tunisia. It is usually made with hot chile peppers, caraway, coriander, cumin, garlic, and olive oil. Harissa sauce is powerful and should be used sparingly. It is often paired with couscous, but is also used to flavor soups and stews. Harissa sauce is simple to make, and is also available from supermarkets.

Rice

Cheap, nutritious, and very easy to cook, rice is a great accompaniment to any Asian stockpot dish. Although there are literally hundreds of different types of rice, there are only 2 basic grains—long and round. Round rice is stirred during cooking to release the starch and produces a creamy, slightly sticky rice, which is perfect for milk desserts, risottos, or sushi. Long grains stay separate and should be washed well before using and not stirred during cooking.

Cooking rice

There are two very good methods of boiling long-grain rice:

1 Bring a large pan of salted boiling water to a boil. Tip in the rice, stir once and simmer fairly rapidly, uncovered, until tender. Drain and turn out on to a large plate for 2 minutes to let the grains dry and separate.

2 After weighing the rice, tip it into a measuring pitcher or a mug and take note of the volume before transferring to a pan. Now measure twice that volume in cold water and add to the pan with a teaspoon of salt. Bring to a boil, lower the heat to a slow simmer, cover tightly, and cook for 15 to 20 minutes for long-grain rice, 10 minutes for basmati, and 30 to 35 minutes for brown rice.

Long-grain rice

This is a polished rice that, like most other white rice including risotto and basmati, has had its husk and bran removed. It can be boiled using either of the two cooking methods just described.

Sushi or Japanese rice

This is a small, round grain that becomes very sticky when cooked, which makes it ideal for shaping into sushi. There are different ways of cooking this kind of rice—some people believe in prewashing, others in presoaking, others in letting the rice stand after cooking. Since each variety of grain differs, it is best to follow the cooking instructions on the packet.

Basmati rice

This is a very delicate, long, slim, fragrant grain, which is used extensively in Indian cooking. It should be washed very well several times and then soaked in warm water for 20 minutes before cooking. After soaking, it must be handled carefully because the grains are fragile and can easily break. Cook the rice by either of the methods described above for just 10 minutes, or use it for aromatic pilaf or spiced rice dishes.

Rice and noodles

Soba

These noodles are a Japanese specialty. They are made with buckwheat flour, which gives them a distinctive flavor. They tend to be of medium thickness.

Thread noodles

These are very thin noodles, which are particularly good with creamy or coconut-based sauces. There are many variations on this noodle: some are made from rice flour and are known as "cellophane noodles" or "rice sticks." There are also Chinese-style thread egg noodles. The Japanese call them *somen* and the Italians call them *vermicelli*.

Egg noodles

Chinese-style egg noodles come in a variety of thicknesses. They can be bought dried in most supermarkets and fresh in specialty stores. Known in Japan as *ramen* noodles, these are the kind most often used in soup bases.

Noodles

All noodles can be stir-fried or served in soup, but it is very important to cook them first.

Cooking noodles

If you are using dried noodles, serve around scant 1 cup per portion dried weight, and for fresh serve 1½ cups per portion raw weight. When cooked, both amounts will yield about 2 cups—although this will vary slightly depending upon the thickness of the noodle and the flour used. As with pasta, noodles should be cooked in a large pan of lightly salted water, with enough room to move around freely. Cook them until tender but still firm to the bite (for a cooking time refer to the package instructions), then rinse well in cold water to remove the excess starch and to stop them from cooking any longer. If the noodles are cooked in the broth they are going to accompany, they will absorb much of the liquid and the starch will thicken the remainder, giving a cloudy soup.

Udon

These are large, white Japanese noodles made from wheat flour. They are usually sold dried. The Chinese and Thais have varieties of wide noodles made from rice flour that can be used in place of udon noodles. These are available fresh in specialty stores.

For this recipe you will need two fondue pots, one in which to keep the hollandaise warm and a second to use as a stockpot for cooking the asparagus and eggs.

Begin by making the hollandaise sauce. Place the egg yolks in a heatproof bowl with two tablespoons of water, and place it over a pan of simmering water on a stove. Whisk until thick and frothy, then turn off the heat, and gradually beat in the melted butter to make a foamy sauce. Whisk in the lemon juice, cayenne pepper, and salt, then transfer to a fondue pot on the lowest heat to keep warm.

In the second fondue pot, stir the lemon juice into the stock, and bring to a boil. Add the asparagus and cook for 4 minutes, until tender. Lift out the asparagus with a slotted spoon and divide it between four plates. Using a fondue fork, swirl the stock so that it is quickly moving in a clockwise direction, then gently crack an egg into the vortex in the center. Cook gently for 2 to 3 minutes, until set. Lift it out and place on top of one of the plates of asparagus. Cook the remaining eggs in the same way and divide them between the other three plates.

Spoon the frothy hollandaise sauce over the asparagus and eggs, season, and sprinkle over the Parmesan cheese. Serve immediately while hot.

Poached eggs and asparagus
with hollandaise sauce

Serves 4

- JUICE OF 2 LEMONS
- 2½ CUPS HOT VEGETABLE STOCK, FOR POACHING (SEE BASIC STOCKS, PAGES 36 TO 37)
- 20 LARGE ASPARAGUS SPEARS
- 4 EGGS
- SALT AND FRESHLY GROUND BLACK PEPPER
- FRESHLY GRATED PARMESAN CHEESE, TO SERVE

For the hollandaise sauce

- 2 EGG YOLKS
- 8 OUNCES (2 STICKS) UNSALTED BUTTER, MELTED
- JUICE OF 1 LEMON
- ¼ TEASPOON CAYENNE PEPPER
- ½ TEASPOON SALT

Tantalizing aromas to whet the appetite

Thai-style duck stockpot

Place the lemongrass on a cutting board and crush it with a rolling pin, until split and slightly flattened. Put it in a fondue pot with the curry paste, cilantro, coconut milk, stock, soy sauce, sugar, and salt and bring to a boil. Add the duck and cook for 4 minutes, then add the vegetables and cook for another 2 to 3 minutes, until tender.

Lift out the duck and vegetables, divide among four bowls, and stir in the basil and sesame seeds. Serve with the noodles or rice, and the lime wedges.

Serves 4

- 1 STALK LEMONGRASS
- 1 TABLESPOON THAI RED CURRY PASTE
- HANDFUL FRESH CILANTRO
- 1¾ CUPS CANNED COCONUT MILK
- 2½ CUPS HOT VEGETABLE STOCK (SEE BASIC STOCKS, PAGES 36 TO 37)
- 2 TABLESPOONS DARK SOY SAUCE
- 1 TEASPOON SUPERFINE SUGAR
- ½ TEASPOON SALT

For the table
- TWO 5-OUNCE DUCK BREASTS, SKINNED AND CUT INTO STRIPS ½ INCH WIDE
- 2 LARGE CARROTS, CUT INTO MATCHSTICKS
- BUNCH SCALLIONS, THICKLY SLICED
- 7 OUNCES BEAN SPROUTS

To serve
- HANDFUL FRESH BASIL LEAVES, ROUGHLY TORN
- 1 TABLESPOON SESAME SEEDS, TOASTED
- COOKED CELLOPHANE NOODLES OR RICE
- LIME WEDGES

Skewered chicken spirals

Place the scallions, garlic, ginger, and soy sauce in a small bowl and mix together well. Set aside for 30 minutes to 1 hour.

Spoon the scallion mixture over the chicken breasts and then roll up tightly lengthwise. Push toothpicks widthwise through the chicken rolls at 1-inch intervals. Using a sharp knife, cut down between the toothpicks to give cylindrical sections of chicken, each pinned in place with a toothpick.

In a fondue pot, very gently poach the chicken in the stock for 8 to 10 minutes, until cooked through. Lift it out with a slotted spoon, and serve with snow peas, boiled rice, and a dash of soy sauce.

Serves 4

- 4 SCALLIONS, FINELY CHOPPED
- 2 GARLIC CLOVES, FINELY CHOPPED
- 2-INCH PIECE FRESH GINGERROOT, CHOPPED
- 2 TABLESPOONS DARK SOY SAUCE, PLUS EXTRA TO SERVE
- 4 BONELESS, SKINLESS CHICKEN BREASTS
- 2½ CUPS HOT CHICKEN STOCK, FOR POACHING (SEE BASIC STOCKS, PAGES 36 TO 37)
- COOKED SNOW PEAS AND BOILED RICE, TO SERVE

Place the flour, eggs, and salt in a food processor. Pulse until the mixture forms a soft dough. Knead for 2 to 3 minutes, then cover with plastic wrap. Chill for 20 minutes.

Meanwhile, make the infused oil. Place the 2 halved garlic cloves in a very small pan with the olive oil and place on the stove over the lowest heat for 15 minutes, without coloring. If the garlic begins to brown, switch off the heat, and let the garlic infuse in the heat of the oil. Let the oil cool slightly, then remove and discard the garlic. Stir the tomato, basil, and lemon juice into the oil and season to taste. Let cool completely but do not refrigerate.

Place the shrimp, lemon rind, chopped garlic clove, chile pepper, and chives in a clean food processor. Process until very finely chopped. Add the cream and plenty of seasoning, and process again to form a very thick purée.

Using a pasta machine, roll out the dough as thinly as possible. Using a 3-inch cookie cutter, stamp out 32 circles. Place a teaspoon of shrimp filling on each of 16 circles, then cover with the remaining circles. Moisten the edges with water and press together tightly to seal, trying to exclude as much air as possible.

Poach the ravioli in gently simmering water in a fondue pot for 2 to 3 minutes, until they rise to the surface. Using a slotted spoon, remove them from the fondue pot and drizzle with the infused oil.

Jumbo shrimp ravioli
with infused oil

Serves 4

- 3 cups strong all-purpose flour
- 2 eggs
- 1/2 teaspoon fine salt
- 12 raw jumbo shrimp, peeled and deveined
- Grated rind of 1 lemon
- 1 garlic clove, chopped
- 1 small, red chile pepper, seeded and sliced
- 3 tablespoons chopped fresh chives
- 2 tablespoons heavy cream
- 2 1/2 cups boiling, lightly salted water, for poaching

For the infused oil
- 2 garlic cloves, halved
- 6 tablespoons olive oil
- 1 tomato, skinned, seeded and finely diced
- 1 tablespoon chopped fresh basil
- 1 tablespoon fresh lemon juice
- Salt and freshly ground black pepper

Mixed won ton

Won ton are marvelous little dumplings that are traditionally cooked and served in clear chicken broth. The main ingredient used for the filling can be chicken, pork, shrimp, or a mixture, like the one here.

Place the pork and chicken in a bowl and stir in the water chestnuts, scallions, saké, cornstarch, superfine sugar, sesame oil, and plenty of seasoning. In a separate bowl, beat the egg white until stiff and then fold into the pork mixture.

Place a small spoonful of the mixture in the center of each won ton skin and pinch the center together to enclose the filling.

Put the won ton and hot stock in a fondue pot. Add the mushrooms and scallions and cook for 2 to 3 minutes. Lift out the won ton and vegetables. Serve with freshly cooked rice or noodles, and a ladleful of broth.

Serves 4

- 3½ OUNCES GROUND PORK
- 1 LARGE CHICKEN BREAST, FINELY CHOPPED
- 4 CANNED WATER CHESTNUTS, FINELY DICED
- 4 SCALLIONS, FINELY CHOPPED
- 2 TABLESPOONS SAKÉ (JAPANESE WINE)
- 1 TABLESPOON CORNSTARCH
- ½ TEASPOON SUPERFINE SUGAR
- ½ TEASPOON SESAME OIL
- 1 EGG WHITE
- 20 WON TON SKINS
- SALT AND FRESHLY GROUND WHITE PEPPER

For the table

- 2½ CUPS HOT FRESH CHICKEN STOCK OR DASHI, FOR POACHING (SEE BASIC STOCKS, PAGES 36 TO 37)
- FRESH SHIITAKE (GOLDEN OAK) MUSHROOMS, SLICED
- 8 SCALLIONS, SLICED
- COOKED RICE OR CELLOPHANE NOODLES, TO SERVE

WON TON SKINS
You will need to buy won ton skins to make this recipe. They are available from Asian supermarkets and are inexpensive, but if you cannot find them, the recipe will work equally well if you try it with the dough used for the Pot sticker dumplings (see page 47).

3
Sizzlers

Sizzlers offer perhaps the most exciting way to serve fondue. The endless range of tasty morsels in clever packages and crispy coatings offers a thrilling combination of tastes and textures. The food cooks rapidly in the hot oil, so most of these dishes offer quick results. For a crisp, golden result, the cooking oil must be hot enough. Test the oil temperature with a cube of bread first—it should turn golden within 30 seconds—and have plates lined with paper towels for draining the food. Serve dipping sauces in individual bowls. The best oil for sizzlers is peanut oil, which has a delicate flavor. Soybean oil is also good. Oils with a low smoke point, such as olive oil, corn oil, and sunflower oil, are not recommended.

- **Satay vegetable packages** • Packaged scallops • Tempura with sweet soy dip • **Vietnamese-style spring rolls** • **Cheese doughballs** • Molten cheese cubes • Fondue bourguignonne • Sizzling squid with salsa verde • **Eggplant bhajia** • **Lamb patties** • Crispy salmon strips with tomato and tarragon salsa

Satay vegetable
packages

Place the peanuts in a food processor and process until finely chopped. Transfer to a bowl and mix with the carrot, snow peas, creamed coconut, and Worcestershire sauce.

Divide the mixture between eight 4½-inch waxed paper circles, then fold them in half to make semi-circles. Fold over the edges, crimping them tightly with your fingers to enclose the filling.

Deep-fry the packages for 3 to 4 minutes in hot oil in a fondue pot, until the vegetables are tender.

Serves 4

- 2 OUNCES SALTED PEANUTS
- 1 LARGE CARROT, CUT INTO MATCHSTICKS
- 2¾ OUNCES SNOW PEAS, QUARTERED LENGTHWISE
- 2 OUNCES CREAMED COCONUT, COARSELY GRATED
- 1 TABLESPOON WORCESTERSHIRE SAUCE
- PEANUT OR SOYBEAN OIL, FOR DEEP-FRYING

Serves 4

- 2 SHEETS PHYLLO PASTRY
- 1 TO 2 TABLESPOONS GARLIC MAYONNAISE
- 8 LARGE SCALLOPS, SHELLED
- 1/2 LEMON
- 8 LARGE, FRESH BASIL LEAVES
- 8 LONG, FRESH CHIVES
- SALT AND FRESHLY GROUND BLACK PEPPER
- PEANUT OR SOYBEAN OIL, FOR DEEP-FRYING
- SWEET CHILI SAUCE, TO SERVE

Packaged scallops

Cut each sheet of phyllo pastry into four 6-inch squares. Place a small spoonful of mayonnaise in the center of each square and put a scallop on top. Squeeze over a little lemon juice, season with salt and pepper, and top with a basil leaf.

Moisten the edges of the pastry with a little water and fold over to enclose the filling, making a neat, square package. Wrap a chive around each package and gently tie a knot in the center to secure; trim the ends with kitchen scissors.

Cook the squares in hot oil in a fondue pot for 2 minutes, until crisp and golden. Drain on paper towels and serve immediately with sweet chili sauce for dipping.

Serves 4

- 8 RAW JUMBO SHRIMP
- 1 RED BELL PEPPER, SEEDED AND CUT INTO STRIPS
- 1/2 SMALL EGGPLANT, THINLY SLICED DIAGONALLY
- 1 ZUCCHINI, THICKLY SLICED DIAGONALLY
- 1 SMALL SWEET POTATO, THINLY SLICED DIAGONALLY
- 1 LARGE CARROT, THICKLY SLICED DIAGONALLY
- 2 EGG YOLKS
- 4 TABLESPOONS ALL-PURPOSE FLOUR
- 5 TABLESPOONS ICE-COLD WATER
- PEANUT OR SOYBEAN OIL, FOR DEEP-FRYING
- COOKED STICKY JAPANESE RICE, AND PICKLED GINGER, TO SERVE

For the sweet soy dip

- 4 TABLESPOONS DARK SOY SAUCE
- 2 TABLESPOONS CLEAR HONEY
- 1 TABLESPOON CHOPPED FRESH CILANTRO

Tempura
with sweet soy dip

For good, crisp tempura, ensure that the water is ice-cold and that the batter is whisked only very briefly. Unlike many other batters, tempura batter does not improve on resting and must be used immediately.

Peel the shrimp, leaving the tail section intact. Run the tip of a small, sharp knife across the back of each shrimp and pull out and discard the dark intestinal tract.

Dust the shrimp and sliced vegetables with two tablespoons of the flour, shaking off any excess.

Put the remaining flour, the egg yolks, and water in a large bowl. Whisk briefly with a fork to make a lumpy batter. Dip the shrimp and vegetables in the batter; deep-fry in hot oil in a fondue pot for 3 to 4 minutes, until crisp and golden.

To make the soy dip, stir together all the ingredients in a bowl and pour into four small bowls, one for each person.

Drain the tempura well and serve with the sweet soy dip, sticky rice, and pickled ginger.

PICKLED GINGER

Young, fresh gingerroots pickled in sweet vinegar are used in Japanese and Chinese cooking. The ginger is normally pink, although specially pickled red varieties are used with Japanese sushi. Pickled ginger should be drained from the vinegar before use and can be added to many basic dishes for a little extra sparkle. Try shredding some and stirring it through boiled rice with a little fresh cilantro for an interesting accompaniment.

Instant dips

Many sizzlers are crispy, pastry-wrapped or crunchy—perfect for serving with dipping sauces. For those in need of an instant dip, there is a whole host of ready-made, ready-to-eat varieties currently decking grocery shelves:

• Mayonnaise— a squeeze of lemon juice or a crushed clove of garlic makes a delicious instant dip from mayonnaise • Tomato salsa—available in jars or sold fresh • Plum sauce—the ideal accompaniment for Asian-style sizzlers • Mango chutney—provides a good, tropical flavor • Sweet chili sauce—this thick, sweet sauce with a hint of chile pepper is sold in jars • Peking sauce—an Asian sweet and savory sauce, often served with crispy duck pancakes.

Dipping sauces

Speedy dipping ideas

For people with a little more time, there are plenty of **simple** combinations that will produce **tasty** dipping **sauces** from pantry ingredients:

Crème **fraîche** (see page 84) and chopped chives

• Mayonnaise and **grainy mustard**

• Soy sauce and **sweet sherry** in equal quantities • Pesto and **sour cream** • Crunchy peanut butter, coconut cream, and **Worcestershire sauce**

• Chopped **tomatoes**, Tabasco sauce, and scallions

• Mashed avocado, **lemon juice** and olive oil

• **Plain yogurt** and diced **cucumber**

67

Heat the oil in a wok or large skillet and cook the pork, garlic, chile pepper, and five-spice powder over high heat for 4 to 5 minutes, until well browned. Turn into a bowl and stir in the carrot, scallions, bean sprouts, soy sauce, rice vinegar, and sesame oil. Season with salt and pepper, then mix together well and let cool.

Cut the sheets of phyllo pastry in half lengthwise to give eight strips, about 5 inches wide. Spoon the filling onto one end of each strip, then roll up, tucking in the sides to make a neat, cylindrical shape. Moisten the end of each strip with water and press down to secure.

Deep-fry in hot oil in a fondue pot for 2 to 3 minutes, until crisp and golden. Drain well and serve with crisp lettuce leaves and sweet-and-sour sauce.

Serves 4

- 1 TABLESPOON VEGETABLE OIL
- 5 OUNCES GROUND PORK
- 2 GARLIC CLOVES, FINELY CHOPPED
- 1 RED CHILE PEPPER, SEEDED AND FINELY CHOPPED
- 1 TEASPOON FIVE-SPICE POWDER
- 1 LARGE CARROT, CUT INTO MATCHSTICKS
- 4 SCALLIONS, SHREDDED
- 2¾ OUNCES FRESH BEAN SPROUTS
- 1 TABLESPOON DARK SOY SAUCE
- 2 TEASPOONS RICE VINEGAR (SEE PAGE 68)
- 1 TEASPOON SESAME OIL
- 4 SHEETS PHYLLO PASTRY
- SALT AND FRESHLY GROUND BLACK PEPPER
- PEANUT OR SOYBEAN OIL, FOR DEEP-FRYING
- CRISP LETTUCE LEAVES AND SWEET-AND-SOUR SAUCE, TO SERVE

RICE VINEGAR

Rice vinegars from China are different from the rice vinegars from Japan. Both are made from rice wine but they have different flavors—the Chinese is quite pungent and sharp and the Japanese is a little softer. Try to use the right type of vinegar for the style of dish you are cooking. This is a Vietnamese dish, so it is better to use a Chinese type of rice vinegar. If you cannot find it, use white wine vinegar instead. You can use cider vinegar instead of the Japanese rice vinegar.

These delicious doughballs can also be baked in a hot oven. Serve with a fresh tomato sauce for dipping—try the Tomato and tarragon salsa (see page 79) or the Devil's dip (see page 94).

Cheese doughballs

Serves 8

- 3 CUPS BREAD FLOUR
- ½ PACKAGE RAPID-RISE DRIED YEAST
- 1 TEASPOON SALT
- 1 TEASPOON ENGLISH MUSTARD POWDER (SEE PAGE 21)
- 2 TABLESPOONS CHOPPED FRESH CHIVES
- 2 TABLESPOONS OLIVE OIL, PLUS EXTRA FOR GREASING
- TWO 5-OUNCE BALLS MOZZARELLA, DRAINED
- PEANUT OR SOYBEAN OIL, FOR DEEP-FRYING

Sift the flour into a large bowl. Stir in the yeast, salt, and mustard powder, and then make a well in the center. Add the chives, olive oil, and enough warm water to make a firm dough.

Put the dough on a lightly floured surface and knead for 10 minutes, until smooth and elastic. Grease the surface of the dough by rubbing over a little olive oil, then place in a clean bowl. Cover the top of the bowl with a clean dish towel and leave in a warm place to rise for an hour or until doubled in size.

Cut each ball of mozzarella into 20 even-sized chunks. Tear off a piece of the dough and roll it into a ball. Push a cube of cheese into the center of the ball and pinch the dough together to enclose it. Repeat to make about 40 balls.

Gently deep-fry the dough balls in a fondue pot for 5 to 6 minutes, until golden brown and cooked through. Drain on paper towels and serve immediately.

The oil temperature must be correct. If the oil is not hot enough, the cheese will take too long to crisp and the center will ooze out (a little oozing is okay though). Likewise, if the oil is too hot, the outside will brown while the center of the cheese is still cold. Test the temperature with one or two cubes of cheese before you cook them all.

Molten cheese cubes

Cut the cheese into 3/4-inch cubes. Roll the cubes in seasoned flour, until evenly coated.

In a separate bowl, beat together the egg and basil, then dip the cheese cubes in the mixture. Deep-fry the cubes in a fondue pot for 1 to 2 minutes or until golden. Drain on paper towels and serve immediately.

Serves 4

- 8 OUNCES FIRM CHEESE, SUCH AS CHEDDAR OR MANCHEGO (SEE PAGES 22 TO 23)
- 2 TABLESPOONS SEASONED ALL-PURPOSE FLOUR (FLOUR SEASONED WITH SALT AND PEPPER)
- 1 EGG
- 1 TABLESPOON VERY FINELY CHOPPED FRESH BASIL
- PEANUT OR SOYBEAN OIL, FOR DEEP-FRYING

fondue bourguignonne

This is a classic Swiss fondue that is probably the original sizzler. Choose a selection of meats that suit your own tastes and offer a variety of shapes and textures, such as the ones suggested here.

Spear the meat with fondue forks and deep-fry in a fondue pot for 2 to 4 minutes, depending on the size of the pieces.

Put the cooked meat on platters and pass around to your guests. Serve each platter with freshly cooked french fries and a small bowl of dipping sauce.

Serves 4

- 2¹⁄4 POUNDS MIXED MEAT, SUCH AS MINI SPARE RIBS, OR BITE-SIZE PIECES OF CHICKEN, BEEF, OR LAMB
- PEANUT OR SOYBEAN OIL, FOR DEEP-FRYING

To serve
- A SELECTION OF DIPPING SAUCES (SEE PAGES 66 TO 67)
- FRESHLY COOKED FRENCH FRIES (SEE PAGE 15)

SUCCESSFUL SIZZLING

Food cooked at the correct temperature will be crisp on the outside, and succulent on the inside. If the oil is not hot enough, the food will absorb too much fat and become greasy. If the oil is too hot, the food will burn. The average oil temperature for deep-frying is 375°F, but this differs according to the type of food used. For best results, use a deep-fat thermometer. This has a hook to fit to the side of the pot, avoiding the need to have your hands over the hot oil. Position it when the oil is cool, and wait for it to reach the right temperature before immersing food. Never leave hot oil unattended, and place it in a secure position where it cannot be knocked over.

Sizzling squid with salsa verde

Salsa verde is a classic that has many variations. This one makes a lovely accompaniment to fish and seafood.

To make the salsa, place the chile peppers, scallions, garlic, and capers in a food processor and pulse until roughly chopped. Add the herbs and continue to pulse until finely chopped. Transfer to a serving bowl and stir in the lime rind and juice, and the olive oil. Add salt and pepper to taste, cover with plastic wrap, and chill until ready to serve.

Sift the flour, salt, and cayenne pepper into a bowl. Make a well in the center and add the egg and water. Whisk to make a smooth batter with the consistency of light cream.

Dust the squid with seasoned flour, shake off any excess, then dip in the batter, and deep-fry for 4 to 5 minutes in a fondue pot, until golden and cooked through.

Serves 4

- $2/3$ CUP ALL-PURPOSE FLOUR, PLUS EXTRA FOR DUSTING
- $1/2$ TEASPOON SALT
- 1 TEASPOON CAYENNE PEPPER
- 1 EGG
- $1/2$ CUP PLUS 1 TEASPOON COLD WATER
- $3\frac{1}{2}$ OUNCES PREPARED SQUID, CUT INTO RINGS
- PEANUT OR SOYBEAN OIL, FOR DEEP-FRYING

For the salsa

- 4 MILD, GREEN CHILE PEPPERS, SEEDED AND ROUGHLY CHOPPED
- 6 SCALLIONS
- 2 GARLIC CLOVES
- 2 OUNCES SALTED CAPERS, WELL RINSED
- SMALL BUNCH OF FRESH PARSLEY
- SMALL BUNCH OF FRESH CILANTRO
- GRATED RIND AND JUICE OF 2 LIMES
- 6 TABLESPOONS OLIVE OIL
- SALT AND FRESHLY GROUND BLACK PEPPER

Clever ways to serve exciting sizzlers

Eggplant bhajia

The conventional bhaji is made with onion but eggplant also gives a tasty result.

Thinly slice the eggplant lengthwise, then cut each slice widthwise into thin strips. Place the strips in a colander and sprinkle with 1 tablespoon of salt. Set aside for 5 minutes until the eggplant wilts, then run over with cold water, and pat dry with paper towels.

For the red onion raita, mix together all the ingredients in a small bowl, and season with salt and pepper to taste.

Place the eggplant in a large bowl. Stir in the gram flour, baking soda, superfine sugar, cilantro, lemon juice, and enough sunflower oil to make a thick paste that coats the eggplant strips.

Deep-fry small spoonfuls of the mixture in hot oil in a fondue pot for 5 minutes, until golden brown. Drain well on paper towels and serve with the raita and the mango chutney for dipping.

Serves 4

- 1 LARGE EGGPLANT
- 1 TABLESPOON SALT
- 1 CUP GRAM FLOUR (BESAN)
- 1 TEASPOON BAKING SODA
- 1 TEASPOON SUPERFINE SUGAR
- 2 TABLESPOONS CHOPPED FRESH CILANTRO
- JUICE OF 1 LEMON
- 4 TO 6 TABLESPOONS SUNFLOWER OIL
- PEANUT OR SOYBEAN OIL, FOR DEEP-FRYING
- MANGO CHUTNEY, TO SERVE

For the red onion raita

- SCANT 1 CUP PLAIN YOGURT
- 1/4 CUCUMBER, FINELY CHOPPED
- 1/2 SMALL, RED ONION, FINELY CHOPPED
- 1 TABLESPOON FINELY CHOPPED FRESH MINT OR PARSLEY
- SALT AND FRESHLY GROUND BLACK PEPPER

GRAM FLOUR (BESAN)

This is a superfine flour made from ground garbanzo beans. It is used extensively in Indian cooking and adds the distinctive flavor and yellow color of authentic bhajia. It is inexpensive and can be bought from large supermarkets or specialty ethnic stores.

Adventurous dishes for the ultimate eating experience

Serves 6

- 8 OUNCES LEAN GROUND LAMB
- 4 SCALLIONS, FINELY CHOPPED
- 2 GARLIC CLOVES, FINELY CHOPPED
- 2 TABLESPOONS CHOPPED FRESH PARSLEY
- 2 RED CHILE PEPPERS, SEEDED AND FINELY CHOPPED
- 2 OUNCES FRESH WHITE BREADCRUMBS
- 1 EGG, BEATEN
- SALT AND FRESHLY GROUND BLACK PEPPER
- ALL-PURPOSE FLOUR, FOR DUSTING
- PEANUT OR SOYBEAN OIL, FOR DEEP-FRYING

Lamb patties

Put the lamb, scallions, garlic, parsley, chile peppers, and beaten egg in a large bowl, and mix until well blended. Season generously with salt and pepper.

With floured hands, shape the mixture into 18 small balls, then flatten each with the palm of your hand to form small cakes. Deep-fry in hot oil in a fondue pot for 2 to 3 minutes, until well browned and cooked through but still tender.

Crispy salmon strips
with tomato and tarragon salsa

To make the salsa, put the tomatoes, garlic, red onion, tarragon, olive oil, and lime juice in a bowl and stir together. Season to taste, cover with plastic wrap, and set aside at room temperature for at least 1 hour.

Cut the salmon tail widthwise into thin strips and brush with the lemon juice. Season generously with salt and pepper, then dust with the cornstarch. Deep-fry in hot oil in a fondue pot for 1 minute only, drain, and serve with baby lettuce leaves and the tomato and tarragon salsa.

Serves 4

- 7 OUNCES SALMON TAIL, SKINNED
- JUICE OF 1 LEMON
- 2 TABLESPOONS CORNSTARCH
- SALT AND FRESHLY GROUND BLACK PEPPER
- PEANUT OR SOYBEAN OIL, FOR DEEP-FRYING
- MIXED BABY LETTUCE LEAVES, TO SERVE

For the salsa

- 4 LARGE, RIPE TOMATOES, SKINNED, SEEDED, AND FINELY DICED
- 1 GARLIC CLOVE, FINELY CHOPPED
- 1/2 SMALL, RED ONION, FINELY CHOPPED
- 1 TEASPOON CHOPPED FRESH TARRAGON
- 2 TABLESPOONS OLIVE OIL
- JUICE OF 1 LIME

4

Savory
sauces

If you prefer
to use your fondue pot
for serving sauces rather than
sizzlers or stockpots, there is no need
to stop at the more traditional cheese-
based variety, because there are many
marvelous savory sauces that are ideal for
the fondue pot. From rich tomato sauces to
satisfying cream-based concoctions, and
hot, spicy dips to flavorsome salsas,
there is a full array of tantalizing
sauces that can be made, kept
warm, and served at
the table.

Mixed mushroom fondue • **Beet and crème fraîche fondue** • Bell pepper and tomato fondue • Spicy dal • **Bagna cauda** • Chile pepper and tomato fondue • **Mexican bean salsa** • Smoky barbecue sauce • **Devil's dip** • Satay sauce

Mixed mushroom fondue

Serves 4

- 1½ ounces dried cèpes (also known as porcini mushrooms or boletes)
- ⅔ cup boiling water
- 2 tablespoons olive oil
- 2 garlic cloves, crushed
- 3½ ounces brown or white chestnut mushrooms, thinly sliced
- ⅔ cup marsala wine
- 5 ounces mascarpone (see page 101)
- 2 tablespoons chopped fresh parsley
- Salt and pepper
- 8 cups hot ravioli, tortellini, or potato gnocchi, to serve

Place the cèpes in a small, heatproof bowl and pour over the boiling water. Set aside for 20 minutes to soak.

Heat the olive oil in a fondue pot and cook the garlic and sliced brown or white mushrooms for 5 minutes, until softened and golden. Pour in the marsala wine and cook rapidly for 2 minutes.

Strain the cèpes and add the soaking liquid to the fondue. Finely chop the cèpes and add them to the fondue with the mascarpone. Cook gently, stirring, until the cheese melts. Stir in the chopped parsley and season to taste.

Serve with the hot ravioli, tortellini, or gnocchi, for dipping.

Beet
and crème fraîche fondue

Heat the oil in a fondue pot and cook the cumin seeds for 1 to 2 minutes, until they begin to splutter and pop. Add the shallot and garlic and cook for another 3 to 4 minutes, until tender.

Stir in the crème fraîche, beet, and salt and pepper to taste. Heat through gently, then sprinkle over the chopped chervil or parsley.

Serves 4

- 1 TABLESPOON OLIVE OIL
- 1 TEASPOON CUMIN SEEDS
- 1 SHALLOT, FINELY CHOPPED
- 2 GARLIC CLOVES, FINELY CHOPPED
- 1¾ CUPS CRÈME FRAÎCHE (SEE PAGE 22 FOR SUPPLIERS OR, TO MAKE YOUR OWN, SEE BELOW)
- 3½ OUNCES PLAIN COOKED BEET, VERY FINELY DICED
- SALT AND PEPPER
- 2 TABLESPOONS CHOPPED FRESH CHERVIL OR PARSLEY, TO GARNISH

home-made crème fraîche

Take 2 cups heavy whipping cream and 4 tablespoons buttermilk, and combine in a glass container. Cover and let stand at room temperature (about 70 to 80°F) for 8 to 24 hours, or until very thick. Stir well again, cover tightly, and refrigerate. It will keep in the refrigerator for up to 10 days.

- **6** TABLESPOONS OLIVE OIL
- **4** RED BELL PEPPERS, SEEDED AND CUT INTO THIN STRIPS
- **2** GARLIC CLOVES, FINELY CHOPPED
- **4** PLUM TOMATOES, ROUGHLY CHOPPED
- **⅔** CUP VEGETABLE STOCK
- HANDFUL FRESH BASIL, CHOPPED
- JUICE OF **½** LEMON
- SALT AND PEPPER
- GARLIC BREAD, TO SERVE

Velvety
bell pepper and tomato
fondue

Heat half the olive oil in a fondue pot and gently cook the bell pepper strips for 15 minutes, until very tender.

Add the garlic, chopped tomatoes, and the remaining oil, and cook for another 8 minutes, until the tomatoes are pulpy. Stir in the stock and simmer gently for 15 minutes.

Using a hand-held electric blender, purée the mixture to make a velvety-textured sauce. Stir in the basil, lemon juice, and plenty of seasoning. Serve with pieces of warm garlic bread, for dipping.

Spicy dal

Heat the oil in a fondue pot and cook the chopped ginger, shallot, garlic, and chile peppers for 5 minutes, until softened but not browned.

Stir in the lentils, stock, and curry paste. Bring to a boil and cook gently for 15 to 20 minutes, stirring occasionally, until the lentils are tender and the mixture is thick.

In a separate bowl, dissolve the cornstarch in the lemon juice and stir in the yogurt. Stir the mixture into the dal with the fresh cilantro and flaked almonds. Season to taste and serve with nan bread or pappadams.

Serves 4

- 2 TABLESPOONS SUNFLOWER OIL
- 2-INCH PIECE FRESH GINGERROOT, VERY FINELY CHOPPED
- 1 SHALLOT, FINELY CHOPPED
- 2 GARLIC CLOVES, FINELY CHOPPED
- 2 SMALL, RED CHILE PEPPERS, SEEDED AND FINELY CHOPPED
- 5 OUNCES RED LENTILS
- 2½ CUPS FRESH VEGETABLE STOCK (SEE BASIC STOCKS, PAGES 36 TO 37)
- 1 TABLESPOON HOT CURRY PASTE
- 1 TABLESPOON CORNSTARCH
- JUICE OF 1 LEMON
- SCANT 1 CUP GREEK YOGURT (OR THICK PLAIN YOGURT)
- 2 TABLESPOONS CHOPPED FRESH CILANTRO
- 1 TABLESPOON TOASTED FLAKED ALMONDS
- SALT AND FRESHLY GROUND BLACK PEPPER
- NAN BREAD OR MINI PAPPADAMS, TO SERVE

Serves 4

- 1 TEASPOON BUTTER
- 4 GARLIC CLOVES, FINELY CHOPPED
- 12 ANCHOVIES IN OIL, DRAINED AND ROUGHLY CHOPPED
- 2½ CUPS HEAVY CREAM
- HANDFUL FRESH PARSLEY, CHOPPED
- SALT AND FRESHLY GROUND BLACK PEPPER

To serve
- CHARGRILLED VEGETABLES, SUCH AS ARTICHOKES AND ASPARAGUS
- QUARTERS OF HARD-COOKED EGG

Bagna cauda

This classic Italian dish is usually cooked at the table in a small terracotta fondue pot with a candle burner providing the heat. There are lots of variations but this simple version is delicious.

Heat the butter in a fondue pot and cook the garlic and anchovies for 2 to 3 minutes, stirring to break up the anchovies but without allowing the garlic to color.

Pour in the cream, bring to a boil, and simmer for 5 minutes. Season to taste and stir in the parsley. Serve with chargrilled vegetables and quarters of hard-cooked egg, for dipping.

Savory **sauces** lend themselves to many exciting variations and a wide range of delicious foods may be used as dippers. Alongside the classic **dippers,** such as **bread** and **pickles,** there is an endless **array** of easy-to-prepare and shop-bought tidbits to **entice** and satisfy your dinner guests:

Ready-made dippers

• Grissini breadsticks • Cubes of cured sausage, such as chorizo • Pasta, such as filled tortellini and ravioli • Potato gnocchi • Breadcrumbed onion rings (usually sold frozen) • Tortilla chips • Potato chips • Mini pappadams • Wedges of fruit, such as apple and pear

Quick-dipper ideas

• Cones of salami filled with soft cheese

• Home-made french fries (see page 15) • Baked new potatoes • Roasted vegetables • Spicy potato wedges • French bread croûtons • crispy won ton (see Mixed won ton on pages 58 to 59)—these can be deep-fried for a delicious dipper • Prosciutto, rippled onto skewers • Pieces of toasted pita bread and vegetable crudités • Steamed jumbo shrimp • Steamed vegetables, such as broccoli florets and snow peas

Dipping ideas

Serves 4

- 2 Scotch bonnet chile peppers or other very hot chile peppers, such as habañero
- 2 tablespoons olive oil
- 1 shallot, finely chopped
- 2 garlic cloves, finely chopped
- 1 pound 2 ounces ripe tomatoes, roughly chopped
- ²/₃ cup red wine
- 1 teaspoon balsamic vinegar
- Handful fresh basil leaves, roughly torn
- ½ teaspoon superfine sugar
- Salt and freshly ground black pepper
- Selection of dippers (see pages 88 to 89), to serve

Classic chile pepper
and tomato fondue

This classic sauce can be served with an endless number of dippers, from cooked tortellini and mini ravioli to cubes of cheese, grilled shrimp, and strips of beef.

Skewer the chile peppers with a fork and hold them in the fondue flame, or place under a hot broiler, for 2 to 3 minutes, turning until the chile pepper skins blacken and blister. Using a clean dish towel, rub off the blistered skins. Hold the chile peppers with the fork and slice them open. Scrape out and discard the seeds, then finely chop the flesh.

Heat the oil in the fondue pot and cook the shallot and garlic for 5 minutes, until softened. Add the tomatoes and chile peppers and cook for 5 to 10 minutes, until pulpy. Pour in the wine and balsamic vinegar and cook for another 10 minutes, until slightly thickened.

Stir in the basil and sugar, and salt and pepper to taste. Serve with a selection of dippers.

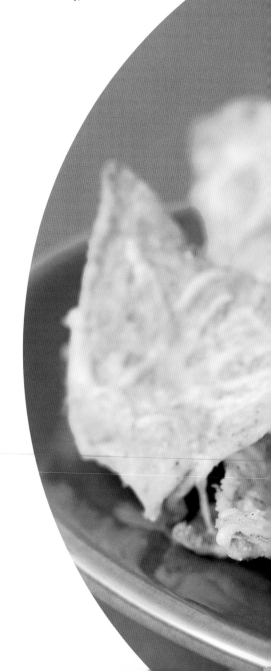

Mexican bean salsa

Heat the oil in a fondue pot and cook the mustard and cumin seeds for 1 to 2 minutes, until they begin to splutter and pop. Add the garlic, shallot, chile peppers, and chili powder, and cook gently for 5 minutes, stirring regularly, until the shallot is softened.

Drain the kidney beans and roughly mash with a fork. Stir into the fondue with the tomatoes and stock. Bring to a boil and simmer for 10 minutes. Stir in the Cheddar cheese and season to taste. Serve with tortilla chips or toasted pita triangles, for dipping.

Serves 4

- 1 TABLESPOON SUNFLOWER OIL
- 1 TEASPOON BLACK OR BROWN MUSTARD SEEDS
- 1/2 TEASPOON CUMIN SEEDS
- 1 GARLIC CLOVE, FINELY CHOPPED
- 1 SHALLOT, FINELY CHOPPED
- 2 GREEN CHILE PEPPERS, SEEDED AND FINELY CHOPPED
- 2 TEASPOONS HOT CHILI POWDER
- 14 OUNCES CANNED RED KIDNEY BEANS, DRAINED
- 14 OUNCES CANNED CHOPPED TOMATOES
- 2/3 CUP HOT VEGETABLE STOCK (SEE BASIC STOCKS, PAGES 36 TO 37)
- 2 OUNCES SHARP CHEDDAR OR OTHER SHARP CHEESE, FINELY GRATED
- SALT AND FRESHLY GROUND BLACK PEPPER
- TORTILLA CHIPS OR TRIANGLES OF TOASTED PITA, TO SERVE

Smoky barbecue sauce

Heat the sunflower oil in a fondue pot and cook the shallot and garlic for 5 minutes, until softened. Stir in the plum tomatoes and tomato purée and cook for 2 to 3 minutes.

Stir in the soy sauce, sherry, orange juice, liquid smoke, sugar, and salt. Bring to a boil and simmer for 10 minutes, until slightly thickened.

Serve with spicy potato wedges and roasted chicken wings.

Serves 4

- 1 TABLESPOON SUNFLOWER OIL
- 1 SHALLOT, FINELY CHOPPED
- 1 GARLIC CLOVE, FINELY CHOPPED
- 4 PLUM TOMATOES, SKINNED, SEEDED, AND ROUGHLY CHOPPED
- 2 TABLESPOONS TOMATO PURÉE
- 1 TABLESPOON SOY SAUCE
- $\frac{2}{3}$ CUP SWEET SHERRY
- $\frac{2}{3}$ CUP FRESH, UNSWEETENED ORANGE JUICE
- 1 TABLESPOON LIQUID SMOKE (SEE ABOVE)
- 1 TABLESPOON LIGHT BROWN SUGAR
- 1 TEASPOON SALT
- SPICY POTATO WEDGES AND ROASTED CHICKEN WINGS, TO SERVE

A wealth of sauces
with heavenly aromas

- 1 POUND 12 OUNCES CANNED CHOPPED TOMATOES
- 4 RED CHILE PEPPERS, THINLY SLICED
- 4 GREEN CHILE PEPPERS, THINLY SLICED
- 2 TABLESPOONS MALT VINEGAR
- 1 TABLESPOON BROWN SUGAR
- 4 TABLESPOONS PEKING SAUCE
- 1/2 TEASPOON TABASCO SAUCE
- SALT AND PEPPER
- SPICY SAUSAGES AND CUBES OF MOZZARELLA, TO SERVE

Devil's dip

This fiery sauce is sure to set your taste buds alight—not a dish for the faint-hearted!

Put the chopped tomatoes into a fondue pot and heat gently. Stir in the red and green chile peppers, vinegar, sugar, Peking sauce, and Tabasco sauce, and bring to a boil. Simmer gently for 15 minutes, then season to taste.

Serve with spicy sausages and cubes of mozzarella, for dipping.

Fiery **sauces** and

deliciously tempting **salsas**

Serves 2

- SCANT 1 CUP UNSWEETENED COCONUT CREAM
- 4 TABLESPOONS CRUNCHY PEANUT BUTTER
- 4 SCALLIONS, FINELY CHOPPED
- 1 TO 2 TABLESPOONS SOY SAUCE
- FEW DROPS TABASCO SAUCE
- 1 TEASPOON SUPERFINE SUGAR
- JUICE OF 1 LIME
- 2 TABLESPOONS CHOPPED FRESH CILANTRO
- 1 OUNCE DRY-ROASTED PEANUTS, FINELY CHOPPED, TO GARNISH

Satay sauce

Satay is a delicious, peanut-based savory sauce from Indonesia. Try serving this version with the Vietnamese-style spring rolls on pages 68 to 69.

Pour the coconut cream into a fondue pot and stir in the peanut butter. Heat gently, stirring until well blended.

Stir in the scallions, soy sauce, Tabasco sauce, sugar, lime juice, and cilantro, and cook for 1 to 2 minutes until piping hot. Sprinkle over the chopped peanuts and serve.

5

Sweet fondues

This chapter is for true fondue fanatics. Each of these recipes has a real air of extravagance and is great for parties, from the dark chocolate sauce served with liqueur-marinated cherries, to the cherry fluff with its melting marshmallows. Not only are there plenty of sweet sauces to choose from, but there are a couple of sizzlers thrown in for good measure, so if you have got two fondue pots, you can go for a double celebration. Keep the napkins handy—it may get a little sticky!

Cherry fluff

• Sizzling chocolate fritters

• **Peaches and cream** • Tiramisu

fondue with sponge drops • Dark

chocolate sauce with marinated cherries

• **Malted banana fondue** • Sticky

toffee sauce • Sparkling strawberry

sauce with shortbread

• **Beignets**

Cherry fluff

Serves 4

- 1¼ cups heavy cream
- 3½ ounces pink marshmallows
- 2 to 4 tablespoons cherry brandy
- Assorted chocolate chip cookies, to serve

Place the cream and marshmallows in a fondue pot and heat gently, stirring until the marshmallows melt. Stir in the cherry brandy. Serve with chocolate chip cookies, for dipping.

Sizzling chocolate fritters

This may sound like a cloying dessert but it is a real treat, especially for birthdays and special occasions. Do not worry if the batter is a little lumpy—it will not affect the delicious result.

In a large bowl, whisk together the milk and egg. Sift in the flour and salt and whisk to make a smooth batter.

Heat the oil in a fondue pot. Deep-fry the candy bars in the oil for 2 to 3 minutes, until crisp and golden. Place on serving plates, dust generously with confectioners' sugar, and serve with a scoop of vanilla ice cream and a sprinkling of chopped nuts.

Serves 4

- 1 cup plus 1 teaspoon milk
- 1 egg
- ⅔ cup all-purpose flour
- Pinch of salt
- Peanut oil, for deep-frying
- 10 miniature candy bars, such as Mars or Milky Way
- Confectioners' sugar, for dusting
- Vanilla ice cream and chopped mixed nuts, to serve

Serves 4

- **14** OUNCES CANNED PEACH HALVES, IN SYRUP
- **1¼** CUPS HEAVY CREAM
- **2** PIECES CANDIED GINGER IN SYRUP, DRAINED AND FINELY CHOPPED
- FEW DROPS VANILLA EXTRACT
- FRESH STRAWBERRIES, FOR DIPPING

Peaches and cream

Place the peaches and their syrup in a food processor and blend to form a smooth purée. Transfer the peach purée to a fondue pot, stir in the cream, and heat gently.

Stir the candied ginger and vanilla extract into the peach mixture. Serve with the strawberries, for dipping.

For the sponge drops
- 3 EGGS, SEPARATED
- $2/3$ CUP SUPERFINE SUGAR
- $2/3$ CUP ALL-PURPOSE FLOUR
- PINCH OF SALT
- CONFECTIONERS' SUGAR, FOR DUSTING

For the fondue
- $2/3$ CUP STRONG COFFEE, BREWED
- $2^3/4$ OUNCES CONFECTIONERS' SUGAR
- $3^1/2$ OUNCES SEMISWEET CHOCOLATE
- 5 OUNCES MASCARPONE (SEE PAGE 22), OR OTHER PLAIN, SOFT CHEESE

Tiramisu fondue
with sponge drops

This recipe uses all the mouthwatering flavors of the classic Italian trifle. If you need to cut back on time, opt for ready-made ladyfingers in place of the sponge drops.

Preheat the oven to 325°F. To make the sponge drops, beat the egg yolks with $2/3$ cup superfine sugar, until pale and thick. In a separate bowl, sift together the flour and salt, then fold half into the egg yolk mixture.

In another bowl, whisk the egg whites until stiff, then fold them into the egg yolk mixture with the remaining flour. Drop spoonfuls onto a lined, nonstick cookie sheet; dust with confectioners' sugar. Bake in the preheated oven for 12 minutes, until lightly golden. Remove from the oven, cool slightly, then transfer to a wire rack.

Pour the coffee into a fondue pot and stir in the confectioners' sugar. Break in the chocolate and heat gently, stirring, until melted. Add the mascarpone and stir until melted. Serve with sponge drops, for dipping.

MASCARPONE
This a creamy, Italian soft cheese, which is used in both sweet and savory dishes. If you cannot find it in your local store, see page 22 for suppliers, or use another plain, soft cheese instead. Before buying, check the packaging to ensure that it is suitable for cooking.

Most of

the recipes in this chapter

have **dipping suggestions** but

here are a few suggestions for **good**

dipping combinations:

Chocolate fondues

- Marshmallows • **Bananas**
- **Nougat** • Toffees • Piped
meringues • **Honey-coated**
nuts • Cubes of toasted
croissant

Creamy fondues

- Chocolate truffles
- **Ladyfingers** • Strawberries
- Raspberries • **Bananas**
- **Fudge** • Marshmallows
- **Chocolate** finger
cookies

Things to dip

Fruity fondues

• Pineapple cubes • Pieces of mango • Slices of kiwifruit • Shortbread wedges • Chocolate truffles • Cape gooseberries (ground cherries) and sweet cherries dipped in melted white chocolate • Pound cake • Whole strawberries

This is a luscious, indulgent dessert that may take a little planning ahead but is well worth the effort. The chocolate sauce can be reheated easily and the brandy reserved from the cherries makes a lovely, warming drink to accompany the fondue.

Using a toothpick, pierce the cherries in several places and put in a large, shallow bowl. Pour over the brandy and let marinate for 12 to 24 hours, turning occasionally.

Strain the cherries, reserving the soaking brandy. Break the chocolate into a fondue pot and add the milk, cream, sugar, and butter. Heat very gently, stirring until the mixture melts into a warm, glossy sauce. Holding the cherries by the stems, dip them into the chocolate sauce.

Dark chocolate sauce with marinated cherries

CHOCOLATE

Chocolate is marvelous. It is luxurious, silky-smooth, and offers a greater feel-good factor than any other single food, so it always pays to choose the best. For cooking purposes, a rich, dark chocolate, such as baking or semisweet chocolate, is ideal—check the label for the cocoa solids content and never go below 50 percent. The best chocolate contains 70 percent and this is now widely available in supermarkets. You can also buy chocolate with a higher percentage than this but, although it is delicious, it can be unstable and difficult to handle when it comes to cooking. Chocolate absorbs odors from other foods, and even soaks up unlikely smells such as cigarette smoke and perfume, so it should be stored separately in a cool, dark place.

Serves 4

- 1 POUND WHOLE, UNPITTED CHERRIES, WITH STEMS
- SCANT 1 CUP GOOD-QUALITY BRANDY

For the chocolate sauce
- 8 OUNCES SEMISWEET CHOCOLATE
- $2/3$ CUP MILK
- $1/3$ CUP HEAVY CREAM
- GENEROUS $1/3$ CUP SUPERFINE SUGAR
- 1 OUNCE ($1/4$ STICK) UNSALTED BUTTER, DICED

Serves 4

- **2 LARGE, RIPE BANANAS**
- **1¼ CUPS MILK**
- **2 TO 3 TEASPOONS MALT SYRUP** (AVAILABLE FROM HEALTH-FOOD STORES)
- **CHOCOLATE TRUFFLES, TO SERVE**

Malted banana
fondue

Peel the bananas and mash well with a fork. Put them in a fondue pot with the milk and malt syrup. Gently heat the mixture, whisking with a hand-held electric blender, until warm and frothy. Serve with chocolate truffles, for dipping.

Sticky toffee
sauce

Place the cream, sugar, butter, and vanilla in a fondue pot. Gently bring to a boil, stirring, until the sugar has dissolved. Lower the heat and serve with strawberries, banana slices, and ladyfingers, for dipping.

Serves 4

- **1¼ CUPS HEAVY CREAM**
- **½ CUP LIGHT BROWN SUGAR**
- **2 OUNCES (½ STICK) UNSALTED BUTTER**
- **FEW DROPS VANILLA EXTRACT**
- **STRAWBERRIES, SLICES OF BANANA, AND LADYFINGERS, TO SERVE**

Irresistible **sweet** fondues for pure **indulgence**

106

Fresh strawberries make a lovely base for this sauce, but this recipe also works very well with other soft fruit, such as raspberries and blueberries.

Preheat the oven to 350°F. To make the shortbread, place all the ingredients in a food processor and pulse until the mixture forms a soft dough. Place the ball of dough on a nonstick cookie sheet and, using the fingertips, press out the mixture until it is 1/2-inch thick.

Prick the shortbread in several places with a fork and bake in the preheated oven for 15 to 20 minutes, until golden. Score into eight wedges and let cool slightly. When firm, transfer to a wire rack. Dust with confectioners' sugar.

To make the strawberry sauce, place the strawberries and confectioners' sugar in a food processor and process together to make a thick purée. Transfer to a fondue pot, stir in the wine, then heat gently.

In a separate bowl, dissolve the arrowroot in the rum and pour into the fondue. Bring to a boil, stirring continuously, until the mixture has thickened. Serve with the shortbread, for dipping.

Sparkling strawberry sauce with shortbread

Serves 4

For the shortbread
- 2/3 CUP ALL-PURPOSE FLOUR
- 1/4 TEASPOON SALT
- 2 OUNCES GROUND RICE OR SEMOLINA
- GENEROUS 1/3 CUP SUPERFINE SUGAR
- 3 1/2 OUNCES (7/8 STICK) UNSALTED BUTTER, DICED
- CONFECTIONERS' SUGAR, FOR DUSTING

For the strawberry sauce
- 1 POUND OF FRESH STRAWBERRIES, HULLED (DESTEMMED) AND HALVED
- 1/2 CUP CONFECTIONERS' SUGAR
- 2/3 CUP SPARKLING WHITE WINE
- 1 TEASPOON ARROWROOT
- 2 TABLESPOONS WHITE RUM

Beignets

The word "beignet" comes from the French word for "fritter." The recipe given here is not for purists because it is based on choux pastry, which is usually baked to make éclairs. When fried, however, it gives a delicious, crunchy exterior with a soft and airy center.

Serves 4

- ⅔ cup all-purpose flour
- 2 ounces (½ stick) unsalted butter, diced, plus extra for greasing
- 1 cup plus 2 tablespoons hot water
  Few drops vanilla extract
- 1 egg yolk
- 2 eggs
- Vegetable oil, for deep-frying
- Strawberry jelly, lemon curd, or chocolate sauce, for filling
- Confectioners' sugar, for dusting

Sift the flour carefully onto a large sheet of waxed paper.

Place the butter in a small pan and pour in the hot water. Bring to a boil, stirring, until the butter has melted.

Tip the flour into the boiling liquid and remove from the heat. Beat with a wooden spoon to make a smooth, thick paste. Add the vanilla extract, then gradually beat in the egg yolk and whole eggs, until the batter is smooth and glossy.

Divide the mixture into four bowls, one for each diner. Heat the oil in a fondue pot. Using buttered spoons, scoop out tablespoons of the mixture and carefully drop them into the sizzling oil. Cook for 5 minutes, until puffed and deeply golden.

Make small pastry bags out of triangles of waxed paper, and fill with warm jelly, lemon curd, or chocolate sauce.

Using a slotted spoon, remove the puff balls from the fondue pot and drain on paper towels. Using a metal skewer, make a hole in the top of each ball and gently squeeze in some of the filling. Dust generously with confectioners' sugar and serve immediately.

index